STRATEGICALLY PLACED
BE THE CHANGE THAT GOD NEEDS

Strategically Placed
Be the Change That God Needs

LaTrina R. Alfred

Scripture quotations marked KJV are from the Holy Bible, King James Version (Authorized Version). First published in 1611. Quoted from the KJV Classic Reference Bible, Copyright © 1983 by The Zondervan Corporation.

Scripture quotations marked NIV are taken from the Holy Bible, New International Version®. NIV®. Copyright © 1973, 1978, 1984 by International Bible Society. Used by permission of Zondervan. All rights reserved. [Biblica]

Print information available on the last page.

Rev. date: 10/27/2016

To order additional copies of this book, contact:
Xlibris
1-888-795-4274
www.Xlibris.com
Orders@Xlibris.com
746907

CONTENTS

Preface vii

Introduction ix

Helps 1: Let them try it 1

Helps 2: Bind the Glass Ceiling 7

Helps 3: The Lies they told, really? 13

Helps 4: They did what? 19

Helps 5: Schemes, Systems and Plans 25

Helps 6: Victimizing 31

Helps 7: Change your environment: Make a Difference 37

Helps 8: Be a Game Changer 45

Preface

Decide today to be the change that God needs in the workplace. You are victorious! Choose to live your life as unto God, giving Him your entire being. It's the enemy's job to use others to try to distract you, to discourage you, and to destroy you. But his tactics, schemes, and devices are bound by the blood of Jesus. Life is not always fair, but one thing we know for sure is that God's word says the favor of God surrounds you daily like a shield. Choose to walk within that shield and watch God move. I know God will slay your Goliath, because He slayed mine. Please choose to know without wavering in your faith that with God all things are possible. But, it is a choice, what will you choose? Nothing shall be withheld from you when you walk upright before God. God promises that He will make your enemy your footstool. He will do just that, but you must walk in Him knowing that He will complete the work in you. So press forward and see the promises of God be expressed in your life. See your great God move mountains and release abundance into your life. See His mighty hand at work. With each distraction give Him praise, with each discouragement give Him glory, and with each victory give Him gratitude. Choose to be the change that God needs in the workplace. You are victorious! Don't let the workplace change you, but you be the change in the workplace.

Introduction

"Blessed be the God and Father of our Lord Jesus Christ, who has blessed us with every spiritual blessing in the heavenly places in Christ," (Ephesians 1:3, NASB). *Have you ever experience trouble in the workplace? Have you ever had people come against you not because you were not doing your job, but because there was something unique or different about you? You were not a follower or a part of their inside group or groups? Have you ever experienced your co-workers treat you like you had the plaque? Have you ever had a time where you felt you were in the fight of your life and that nothing seemed to be going your way? That all arrows were pointing in the favor of your enemy? Well today, I want to encourage you to trust, know, and be it verified that God does exist in the workplace. It may seem like a place that normally does not need God to visit, commune at, or hang out in, but I've come to tell you that you need Him there.*

In life, there are times where you've experience being disliked, disrespected, and discouraged. People on your jobs took you fore granted, walked on your forgiveness, and let the air out of your intestinal fortitude for a weakness. Therefore, people seek ways to try to get rid of you or cause you to get rid of yourself. Which means that a shifting starts to take place and cause you to get out of character, thus giving them probable cause to fire you. Today my sister and my brother I want you to know that God does exist in the workplace and He desires that you be the transformation the environment needs and not allow the enemy to transform you.

From today forward make sure you usher God into your workplace and enjoy the peace, tranquility, and empowerment that will come with it as God overthrows your enemy. Put your armor on and allow God through you to win the battles, win the war.

Thank you to my husband for loving me and supporting me. To my children who love me so much, to my sisters for always saying "Sissy you can do it!", to my grandmother the backbone of our family and to my mom who is the epitome of strength and love.

Helps 1

Let them try it

Workplace Prayer

Father in the name of Jesus, I pray that You would bless this place. Give me laughter and peace. I will go in and possess all that You have for me today.

Hostility, Violence, Anger, Hatred, Intimidation, Unfairness, Lies, and Deceit

In today's world, the workplace has become a strong battleground for the children of God, people in general. People encounter different things and a multiplicity of issues in their eight (8) more or less hours in a workday. You will be going along minding your own business and then boom, there comes a bomb right in your direction. Not a

---

1

fire cracker, but a M80 that causes you to stop in your tracks. But today I caution you to know this, the devil has set people on your job with assignment orders to try and destroy you. Now you see the word used was "try." He does not have the orders to destroy, but to try and destroy. Which means you have something on the inside of you that can stop him and cause you to have the victory. Now think back to your bible, you remember that wheat and tare thing? Yes those wild ones growing up right beside the roses? They want you to quit, leave, lose your temper, or even fail at what you do. The devil wants you to be belittled and embarrassed. He wants you to be left exposed as helpless and unsettled. He wants to put you in a corner with your mouth shut. He wants to taunt and harass you and make think that nobody sees it, believes you, or even cares about what you are going through. He wants you to explode!

He has set traps to try and stop your promotions, your bonuses, tear down your confidence, and halt your upward mobility. He even has the audacity to try to say what you won't get when it comes to your evaluations, job assignments, or promotions. Ha, ha now that is funny. Because as you and I both know promotions come from God and as for bonuses God gives the increase. So I say as long as you've earned it, it shall be yours, because God's word says so. Let them write it down the way they see it, but trust me when it's all said and done God will ensure you get what you deserve, period! Don't allow them to trap you by backing you into a corner and cause you to work in fear, be inferior, or push you out the door. Once on a job I was working on, I was told my supervisor said he was going to get rid of me, cause me to be relocated. Now what he did not know is that the person he was trying to use to sabotage me told me about his ploy. I laughed and told it to God. I want you to know that same person God has caused to be relocated and moved out. As ambassadors for Christ you must know that God guarantees you will win this battle. God promises to fight your battles and He wins, always.

Battle Scripture

For the battle is not yours, but it's God's. 2 Chronicles 20:15 (KJV)

Notes:

Helps 2

Bind the Glass Ceiling

Workplace prayer

Father today I confess that I need You to survive in this place. Others may see me as less, but You see me as the professional that I am and worthy of my hire. In Jesus name. Amen

Glass ceiling is a political term used to describe "the unseen, yet unbreachable barrier that keeps minorities and women from rising to the upper rungs of the corporate ladder, regardless of their qualifications or achievements (www.referenceforbusiness.com).

Hello people, guess what if you are not a majority; you are a minority at least in man's eyes. But with God you are a majority because God is no respecter of person. God gives good and perfect gifts to His children. Worldly people don't see this, but it's true. Trust and believe that those who God has destined to be victorious will be victorious and that includes you! You have already been set up to be blessed. But its all about how you see the blessings of God. Do you pray and get up believing you have what you ask for or do you get up wondering if you have what you have asked for? Get up, go in, and expect the all-inclusive blessings of God. Expect the prayers you have prayed to come to pass. God will never allow you to be short changed, barely get blessed, or have a return to sender. God is not a as they say Indian giver. He does not promise or guarantee a victory and take it back because we fail at our test. Now sometimes we may have to have a retest, but it so that we will learn the materials needed to guarantee we learned how to defeat that enemy. But at the end of the day you will find that your enemy although he seems large is not a match for our God. God's all powerful hand will cause the enemy to give of all his substance to you. But you must be in position and ready to receive the blessings. I use to believe I was a not as good as the men who did the same job as me. But as the years rolled by I saw that I was better at my job than some of the men I worked with. Why, because I felt the challenge and the push from the inside of me. I began to ask God to help me to always advance over my enemy and as I learned I become smarter, I became sharper.

Today I admonish you to confess that you are the majority and believe that God will do exactly what He has promised. He will shatter the glass ceiling for you, but must you walk through it. You must grab ahold of each and every piece that belongs to you. Can you see it coming down, because it is?

Battle Scripture

For the weapons of our warfare are not carnal, but are mighty through God for the pulling down of strongholds. 2 Corinthians 10:4 (KJV)

Notes:

Helps 3

The Lies they told, really?

Workplace prayer

Father today in the name of Jesus, I walk true to Your word knowing that I have done all that I can do. With every lie I pray that you would uncover and prove my case. Father thank you that it's all a lie and that I will be vindicated. In Jesus name. Amen

John 8:44 KJV says, You belong to your father, the devil, and you want to carry out your father's desires. He was a murderer from the beginning, not holding to the truth, for there is no truth in him. When he lies, he speaks his native language, for he is a liar and the father of lies.

People of God, remember that those who tell, build, and start lies on you are of their father the devil. They are working with what is running in their bloodline. They are being used by the devil to do his dirty work. These people need you to influence change in them. They need you to open their eyes and to save them from destruction, because they are speaking their father's native language. They don't understand what they are saying and oftentimes they don't know they are being used to hurt you or set you up. Whether they are male or female Satan will use them. Now ask yourself three things:

1. Are you a Christian?
2. Are you focused?
3. Are you an influencer?

Now examine yourself and see if you are all or some of these. If you are then you must know that God is with you. Being a Christian does not give you a get out of trials and tests free card. Being a Christian places you in direct line of fire to be blessed. You must figure out how you must display the God that lives in you throughout your workplace. You ask the question, is God truly here with me? The answer is YES, He is! In all that we say and do God is right there being an outstanding corner man. I admonish you to be assured that He is, because He said He would never leave us or forsake us.

In this fight you are pushing in prayer trying to remain Christ like and all hell has broken loose. You cannot even tell if you are coming or going. All you know is that you have made it through another day to fight. Although this is naturally said, you will make it because the Spirit of God knows where He is and what to do at all times. But yes we do sometimes feel this way. You've ask yourself what have I done that was wrong? Why me Lord? Why am I going through all of this? In most cases you haven't done anything wrong, it's just the devil on his job. He has been sent on assignment to try to kill, steal, and destroy YOU. You are on the battlefield and you must fight. You must remain focused on the strategy God has strategized for you through His word. Through all the other victories He has won for you.

What's happening to you is there to cause you to lose focus, be distracted, and to be led down a dead end. But know that today brings a different surge and resistance to be felt. Trust and believe that this too shall pass. You will make it through. You will use the word of God as your road map, because you are the influencer. You are the one who has been empowered, gifted, and blessed to see and remove the traps that have been set in your work environment.

It is true you have been lied on, there has been a contract sent out to destroy you, and to add insult to injury you must continue to show respect and let your light shine. Now that sounds crazy and why should I show respect and let my light shine. For those people, for what reason? Well it's because God says to and it's because God is loving and kind, so then we should be also.

Through all of this you must continue to be all things to all people. Openly the enemy has tried to discredit you; therefore openly God will restore you. Psalms 23:5KJV says "thou prepareth a table before me in the presence of mine enemies." Today you have challenges, but I must express to you that you were chosen for this and you shall cross the finish line. Learn the material and pass the test! It's an open book test and you have smartest tutor in the world dwelling on the inside of you. You will not fail because you were commissioned to finish this assignment. You have what it takes to be better and not bitter. Work towards your victory through Christ Jesus the author and finisher of your faith. And it shall be a victory indeed. You have what it takes to get through all this mess and defeat the disparagement in your life. You are built Jesus tough!

Battle Scripture

And God said; Let us make man in our image,

after our likeness. Genesis 1:26 (KJV)

Notes:

HELPS 4

They did what?

Workplace Prayer

Father in the name of Jesus, I decree and declare victory in this place. No longer am I the tail, but the head. I claim all that You have for me in the midst of my enemies today. Thank you for the table You have prepared for me. In Jesus name. Amen

Forget about the lies they told and hold onto and know that good, strong, and awesome things grow through dirt. You are an influencer; not the one being influenced. The key is to go from faith to knowing. The bible says and we know that all things work together for the good (Romans 8:28 KJV). You must know who you serve and what He is capable of. You must have the faith to believe God for change.

You must emphatically, without a shadow of doubt believe that He can and will use you for great change.

After all that you have been through in this life you held on. You remember that God left a resume' of His victories to help you. Isn't it funny that God created us from dirt and that the things we need naturally grow through dirt? So why would dirt stop being a part of your life? No it's an essential part of our lives. As you live and learn you have allowed some dirt to fall throughout your lives. What the world needs is in you and it is because of the dirt you have gone through. You may be dirty, grimy, and soiled, but you have all the nutrients and chemicals to produce good soil, good dirt. You are essential to make a difference. You must allow the dirt of life to grow you and place you into position to receive the blessings and upward movement that will be coming into your life. You cannot stay where you are, you must allow the workplace hostility that has come to make you move. Allow it to push you to grow you to be who God says you are. Stand sure and believe that you are in full bloom. Move from being influenced to be the influencer. You must influence your situation and your surroundings through the word of God. You must cause change to take place right where you are by speaking and doing good things, positive things, and worthy things. You know like grandmother constantly said, "You must say what you mean and mean what you say." You must be who you say you are and display that daily. If you can believe grandmother for what she said when she told you; then what's the problem with believing God for what He says. Don't spend time speaking useless, empty things, but speak worthy things. Change will come and God's mighty hand will move just for you. Trust and believe that God meant what He said when He said, "touch not my anointed, and do my prophet no harm" (1 Chronicles 16:22 KJV).

Battle Scripture

And Deborah said unto Barak, Up; for this the day in which the Lord hath delivered Sisera into thine hand: is not the Lord gone out before thee? So Barak went down from the mount Tabor, and ten thousand men after him. Judges 4:14 (KJV)

Notes;

HELPS 5

Schemes, Systems and Plans

Workplace Prayer

Father in the mighty name of Jesus, show me your will and your way. Allow me to see the enemy's plans, schemes, and strategies. Give me the faith to follow you and miss the ditches dug for me. I am fully dressed for battle through you. In Jesus name. Amen

John 10:10 NIV the thief comes only to steal and kill and destroy; I have come that they may have life, and have it more abundantly.

1. The design
2. The classification
3. The tactics

God help me, an all out assault has been sent my way. How do I strategize? I'm under complete attack. Mayday, mayday can you hear me? I'm being set up. I'm being tried in the fire. Lord I need you!

In the mist of their schemes, systems, and plans God has provided an out strategy to escape the enemy. God has provided a ram in the bush. He has provided through your gifts strength to stand. The power to be victorious. Although the enemy came to stack the odds against you, twist your story, and terminate you those weapons formed shall never prosper. God has given you resources to conquer Satan and move forward. Now I'm not saying that in the midst of all these schemes, systems, and plans that your flesh does not feel this, because it does. Our flesh gets weary and our flesh begins to fight the pain by complaining and desiring to give up. It speaks negative, empty, powerless words into the atmosphere. Stop all the negatism and be assured that you have life and have it more abundantly. The enemy does not understand that what he meant for evil will be used for your success. God has said in Jeremiah 29:11(KJV) "He knows the plans He has for you." God is trying to move you to that prosperous end. But you must have a new mindset that everything that comes against you will be used for your good only. So forget about the schemes, systems, and plans, and walk in victory expecting your abundant and full life. God has given you a powerful battle plan that dictates what you will and will not tolerate. Each and every tactic fits into God's plan and will be used for your greater good. The Lord is my helper. Speak that, believe that, and live that.

<u>Battle Scripture</u>

Though they plot evil against you and devise

wicked schemes, they cannot succeed.

Psalm 21:11 (NIV)

Notes:

Helps 6

Victimizing

Workplace Prayer

Father in the name of Jesus, I know that I am not a victim, but I am a victor. I thank you that my enemy is defeated. In Jesus name. Amen

First Samuel 24:1 KJV says, After Saul returned from pursuing the Philistines, he was told, "David is in the Desert of En Gedi. ² So Saul took three thousand able young men from all Israel and set out to look for David and his men near the Crags of the Wild Goats.

You have been swindled, treated ill, and hoaxed. All these are of the enemy and his mission is to destroy you. You have been chosen as a victim and what's so good about this is that God has allowed this choosing to take place. Why you ask, because you were fabricated for this. You are eligible, equipped, and anointed for all of this. Satan comes to undermine your ability, destroy your character, cut you off from what you know is true and begin to cause you to shut down. He is trying to destroy you and cause you to no longer exist. There's a seek and destroy mission with a sniper rifle pointed straight at all your vital organs. The enemy has pulled the trigger and it has jammed. God won't allow it to be so.

Saul sought after David because he was intimidated. Most of the time we are victimized on the job or in the workplace because of intimidation or inferiority complexes derived from others. You must have the desire to please God and do your job as unto Him and Him alone. Don't try to please man, because we gain favor from man by pleasing God. Bingo that's the key. The people we work with or for do not truly see that we are God's servant, His anointed. Sometimes they do, but don't care. Why, because they are on assignment by the devil.

All they see is that we are in some way a threat to them, to the atmosphere. They lack understanding and they allow the enemy to control them like a puppet on a string. But at the end of the day we have the victory. God will permit a Jehoshaphat victory to come your way. Yes God has allowed all this, but there is a remedy. Jehoshaphat obeyed God and his enemy was confused and killed themselves and left for Johosphat many blessings for him and his people. We have to stand and endure the test knowing that God has a better way of doing things that will expose the enemy and his victimizing. In doing it God's way the enemy shall be defeated. You are anointed for this and you have become stronger inside and out because you have endured this great test. Therefore look in favor of the great blessing to come at the expense of the enemy because you are willing and obedient. You were the victim so they thought, but it has been approved by God to be a blessing to you as the victor.

Battle Scripture

When the going gets rough, take it on the chin

with the rest of us, the way Jesus did.

2 Tim 2:3 (MSG)

Notes:

HELPS 7

Change your environment:
Make a Difference

Workplace Prayer

Father in the name of Jesus, I thank you that this office is blessed, peaceful, and prosperous. You have changed the heart of the king and favor is mine. I am new inside and out. In Jesus name. Amen

Ezekiel 12:2(NIV) Son of man, you are living among a rebellious people. They have eyes to see but do not see and ears to hear but do not hear, for they are a rebellious people.

You have been given orders to change your environment. You have the power and authority to do this through the influence and anointing of God. God wants you to trust Him and He will create opportunity for you to make this change. But you have to do two things. You have to engage your ears and eyes. As you see I did not say mouth. You have to be quick to hear and be watchful. You must be the environment change and not let the environment change you. If you are altered or changed by your environment you develop will a:

1. Defeated attitude
2. Disgruntle attitude
3. Dysfunctional attitude
4. Depressed attitude

First of all "God did not give us the spirit of fear, but of power of love and of a sound mind" (2 Timothy 1:7KJV). Now you must recognize that you are not defeated. You will not walk in fear and you are complete in Him. You were not left behind in the midst of this place to be changed, but to be the change. Now I'm talking about the person who is living according to God's statues and precepts. The one sold out and truly seeking to please God. God has strategically placed you in that environment. God has given you a charge to be used effectively. Daily you need to quote the scripture. This is the day the Lord God has made and I shall rejoice and be glad in it (Psalms 118:24 KJV). Why, because you have already won the victory. It's has been predestined for you. Don't get frustrated and dissatisfy God. Be the satisfaction that God needs you to be. Ecclesiastes 12:14 (KJV) "The end of the matter; all has been heard. Fear God and keep his commandments, for this is the whole duty of man. For God will bring every deed into judgment, with every secret thing, whether good or evil."

Your duty is to fear God and keep His commandments. That's it. Don't be **defeated** or **disgruntle** through your mouth or body language. Speak victory, walk in victory and see your outcome. If you can see it, it shall be established. This is only a test and it will come to an end. "For this light affliction is just for a moment, but will bring about greater joy" 2 Corinthians 4:17 (KJV). God will give you beauty for your ashes and He will cause the atmosphere to change for the good Isaiah 61:3 (KJV). Joy shall come in the morning.

Everything about God operates and functions properly. Anything that is not operating properly is dysfunctional. **Dysfunctionality** is a sign that something has been altered from its original function and that change must take place. Hostile environments did not get that way over night. There was a process set in motion before the above lies, schemes, systems, plans, and victimizing was started. In this God is mighty and you are more than a conqueror. The bible says that every high place will be cast down and brought under subjection to God. We have worked extremely hard for what we have and for what we wanted. The bible says that promotion comes from God not from man. So if they promote someone else over you who do not meet the requirements, it's only a set up for an even greater blessing to come into your life. So what if they rate you lower than what you earned or deserved. Go to God who sees all and knows all. It's only their opinion and not the final say on who you are or what you have done. God will cause the change to be made on your behalf. You just keep on doing your job as unto God and watch God move. I have seen God destroy the enemy throughout my many years of employment and what He has done for one He will do for another. Never has God lost a battle for the battle belongs to the Lord.

You may be undervalued, unappreciated, underpaid, or under-bonused, but you are the person for the job. God has placed you there to get the glory. You are not **depressed**. You are blessed. You have to know that none of these are you, you're above and not beneath. You are the head and not the tail. In Isaiah 61:7 says; For your shame ye shall have double; and for confusion they shall rejoice in their portion: therefore in their land they shall possess the double: everlasting joy shall be unto them. All that has been done will bring double blessings back to you, for the confusion you will rejoice and then you will have everlasting joy because you will remember all that the Lord has done. The king will have to come subject to God. God desires to bless you in the midst of your enemies and they cannot stop this. They tried to kill you. They tried to destroy you. They tried to hinder you. They tried to stop you. But God has given you the victory through all they tried. And since you are in the palm of God's hand they cannot pluck you out because He is in control of them and you. Now, I admonish you to trust God's word and count it all joy because they come against you falsely for His name sake and seal it with electrifying praise. God's got your back and there is nothing the enemy can do about it. While you are waiting on God to change your environment you must form the change needed so that you can prosper. So that God's Spirit has free course. Encourage yourself and say that I'll let nothing separate me from the love of God. God loves you and He will never allow more to come upon you than you can bear. You can bear this because you were built for it and you will conquer this, all of this. Change your atmosphere because you serve the one who made it. He made the entire universe and it must come subject to HIM.

<u>Battle Scripture</u>

The blessing of the LORD, it maketh rich, and he

addeth no sorrow with it. Proverbs 10:22 (KJV)

<u>Notes:</u>

Helps 8

Be a Game Changer

Workplace Prayer

Father in the name of Jesus, Help me to be and remain the person you have created me to be. Lord help me to understand that this battle although I can feel it, it does not belong to me, but to you. Amen

But the Comforter, which is the Holy Ghost, whom the Father will send in my name, he shall teach you all things, and bring all things to your remembrance, whatsoever I have said unto you. John 14:26 (KJV)

God said He did not leave us powerless and as long as we keep our hands up and focus on Him we will have the victory. The battle is won when we listen to God and engage all our efforts towards allowing him to strengthen us.

In American football, the quarterback relays to his teammates in the huddle what play the coach has called. Quarterbacks usually audibilize when he discovers that the defense has guessed correctly and is properly aligned to stop the play. They Holy Ghost sees what's ahead and implements strategy for you to follow. You are put in the game to be a game changer. You are to call an audible in the midst of the set up. Cause a shift in the defense and allow God to realign you. Relax my sister and my brother God is in control and it will be a touchdown every time! You have the power to call an audible through the Spirit of God and the game will be changed, turned around and intercepted for you. God's passes as the quarterback never misses the intended target. He will place it into your hands right when and where you need it.

<u>Battle Scripture</u>

And it came to pass, when Moses held up his hand,

that Israel prevailed: and when he let down his

hand, Amalek prevailed. Exodus 17:11 (KJV)

<u>Notes:</u>

End of the book motivation. Enjoy!

It's yours no matter "WHO"

Many blessings and strength to those who have endured encountered or are experiencing workplace hostility or violence at this time. Those who have endured it through unfairness, lies, schemes, stacking of the team, dislikes, and games that are being played against you because of who you are. To those who do what is right, but are not noticed by man. God has a plan bigger than yours or the people you work with or for. But you have to know this. They are only catapulting you towards your blessings. They are only setting you up to be blessed beyond your and their expectations. Enjoy the ride and give God the credit not the enemy. What I mean is close your mouth to their behavior and sayings, engage your eyes seeing the victories set before you. Come into your workplace already prayed up, praised up and word up. Walk in joy and faith because you can see the promised victory. Send the devil back frustrated, stressed, and angry not you. Satan can only antagonize you. He came to give you many detours in all directions, but they shall never prosper. All you need to do is use all that you have in your bag of rocks and conquer it all. So when they used mediocre people, their friends, and family putting them ahead of you. Have faith to know that if God brought you to it He will bring you through it and with all this He causes great blessings to be placed right before your enemy just for you. You know that table that has been prepared? I'm reminded of a story, there was a woman who was going through so much on her job. The devil thought that he had her with all the key players on his team and all the people or character witnesses he had hustled up. But for her; God decided to truly show that He was God. He slew Goliath for her. Now that's not how the story in the bible went, but this is how God did it for this woman. He took down the enemy with one blow and left the rest of the team players wondering what had happened. God showed them that He was God and they did not stand a chance. There was not one "I" dotted or "T" crossed that God did not put an explanation mark after. The battles won for you will leave nothing but jaw dropping facial expressions within the faces of those left watching. My sister, my brother victory is already yours for the asking. So change your environment by walking in supernatural change and never cease to pray for your enemies. Endure hardness as a good soldier. Stay positive, speak victoriously, and praise God constantly. Keep the faith and know that God will never leave you or forsake you no matter what. Also know that God is in charge not man. Man has limits that God has put upon him. Believe that you are destined for another dimension in God.

Quotes:

Don't be changed into want they you to be, but be the change God has destined you to be.

—L. Renee' Alfred

Great kingdom builders grow through dirt.

-- Bishop Anthony Alfred Sr.

CPSIA information can be obtained
at www.ICGtesting.com
Printed in the USA
BVHW03*1904230318
511443BV00003B/7/P

9 781524 548605